Copyright © 2019 Brain Trainer All rights reserved.

No part of this publication may be reproduced, distributed or transmitted in any form or by any means, including photocopying, recording, or other electronic or mechanical methods, without the prior written permission of the publisher, except in the case of brief quotations embodied in critical reviews and certain other non-commercial uses permitted by copyright law.

Trademarked names appear throughout this book. Rather than use a trademark symbol with every occurrence of a trademarked name, names are used in an editorial fashion, with no intention of infringement of the respective owner's trademark. The information in this book is distributed on an "as is" basis, without warranty. Although every precaution has been taken in the preparation of this work, neither the author nor the publisher shall have any liability to any person or entity with respect to any loss or damage caused or alleged to be caused directly or indirectly by the information contained in this book.

Meet the Pharaoh's Family

Kavi

Henna

Queen Henu

Pharoah Kufu

Kavi, the son of the mighty Pharaoh Kufu, is bored of having to stay in the royal palace all the time. He's decided it's time to go on a secret Egyptian Adventure! Help him avoid the guards and sneak out.

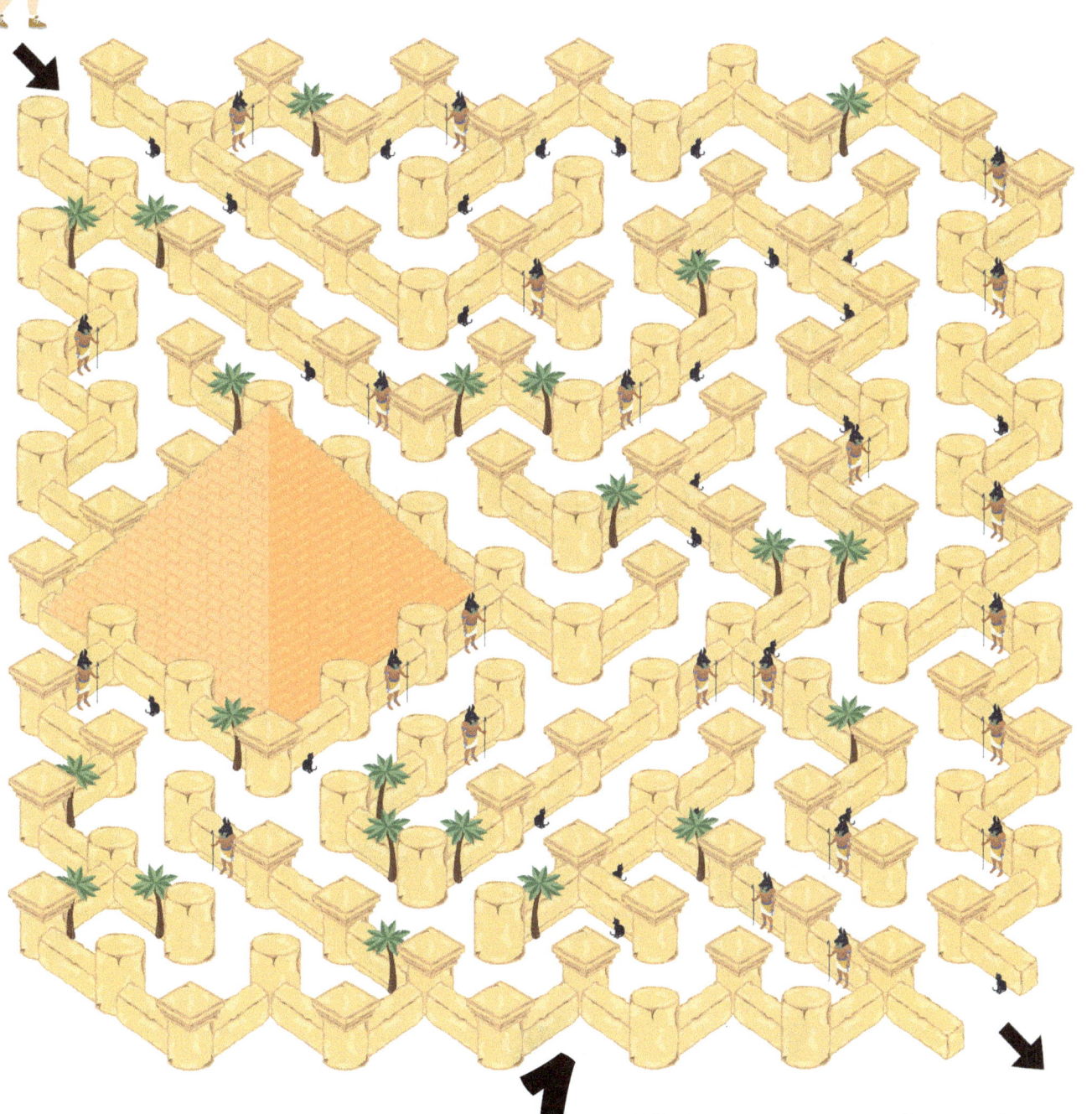

1

Make your way through

The more people the merrier, so Kavi convinces his younger sister Henna to join him too!

2 Climb the ladders

Henna can't go anywhere without her lucky rag doll Nedi though. Help her look around the palace to find it.

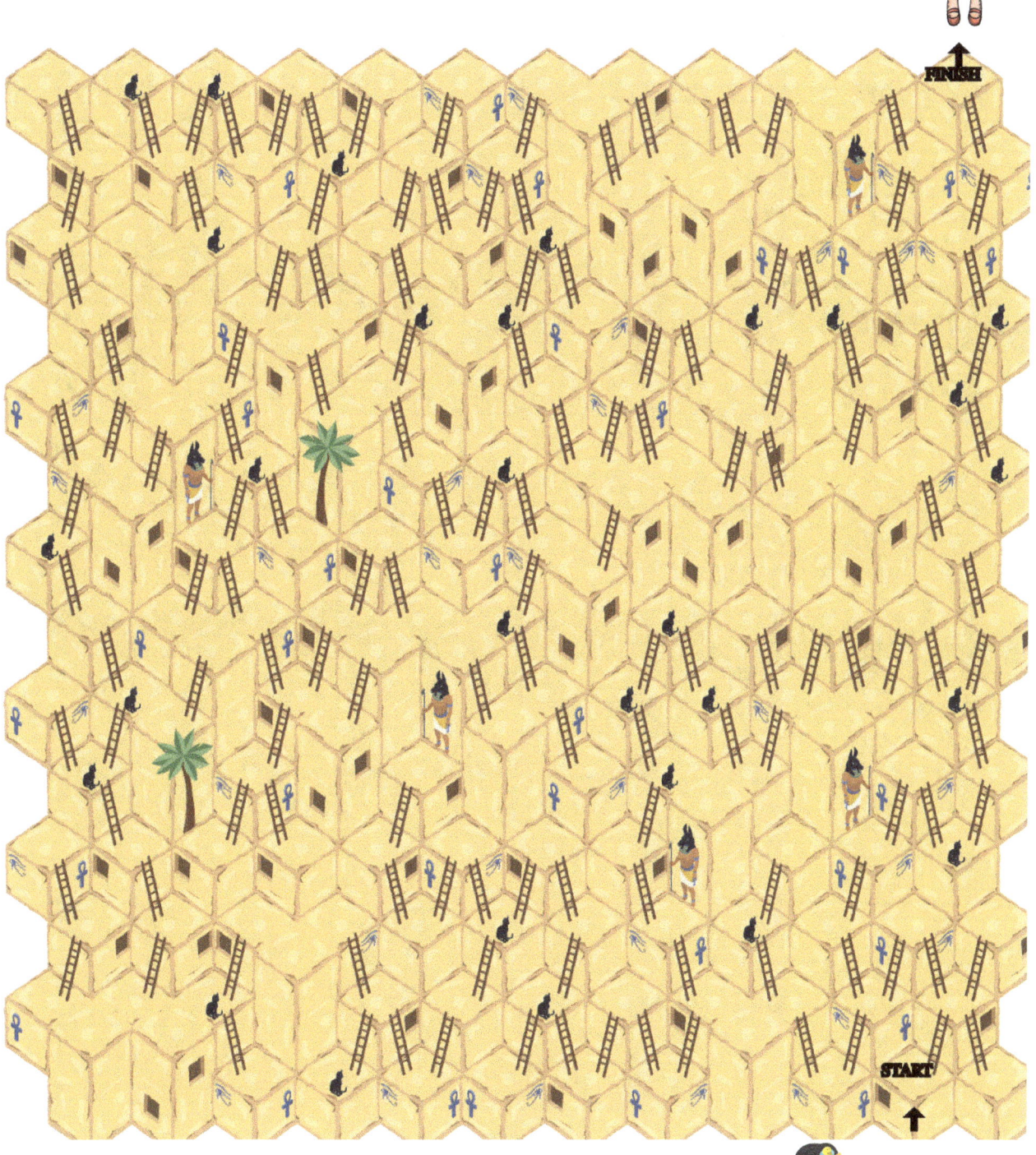

3

Now that you've made it out, the first stop is to the market to stock up on supplies and snacks for the journey. Yum!

Kavi and Henna can't carry everything themselves. Buy a bag first and then go through all the stalls to find what you want.

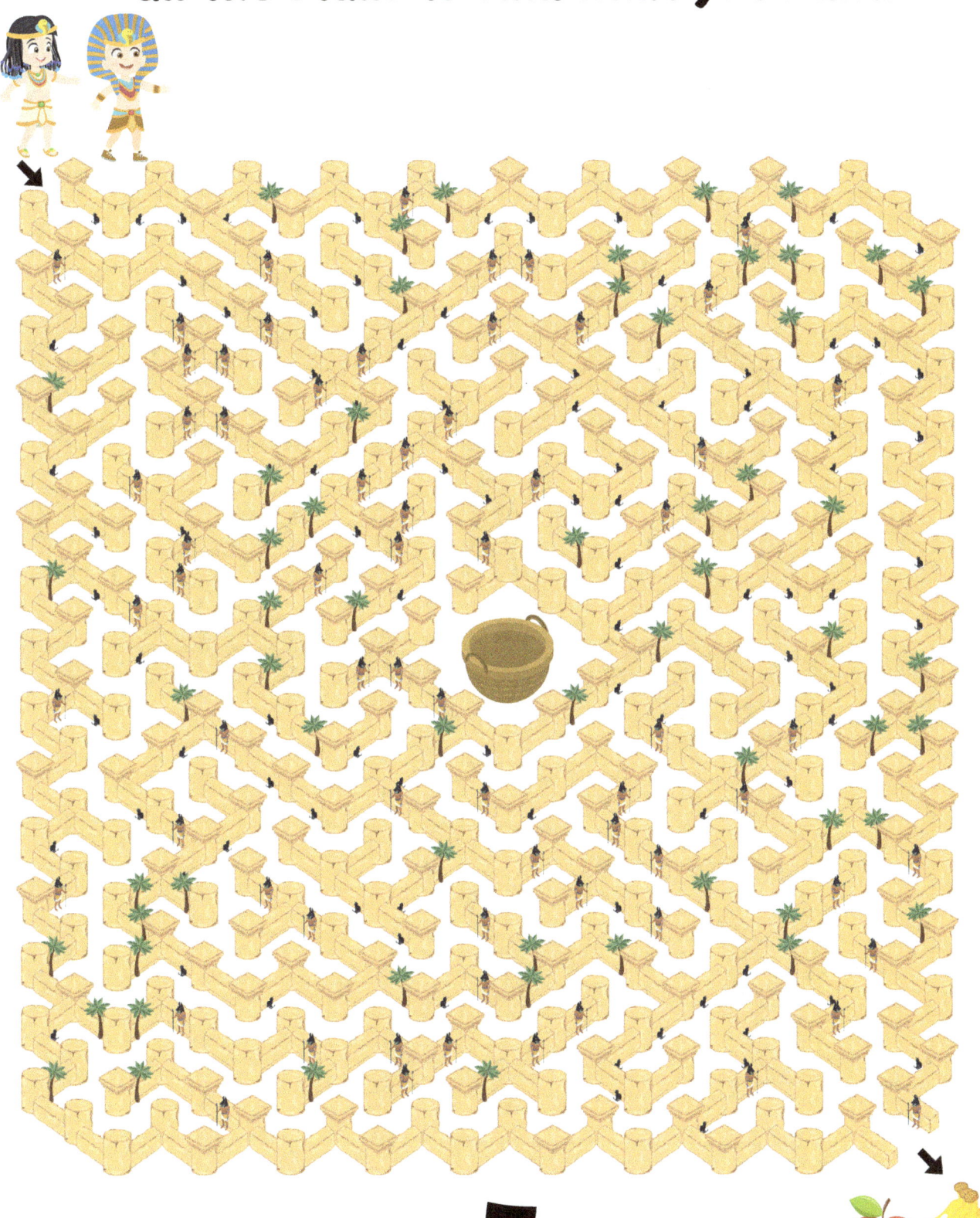

5

Oh no! You see a guard. If he sees Kavi and Henna they'll be in big trouble. Leave the markets without him seeing you.

On the way out, they run into their mum's friend Nala. She lost her special gold necklace back in the market. Help her find it ! Don't forget to stay away from the guard though...

7

Without her necklace, Nala is no longer protected from the evil spirits. Help her avoid the evil spirits until she finds her necklace.

You find the necklace, but it is broken! Help Henna collect all the pieces in her bag.

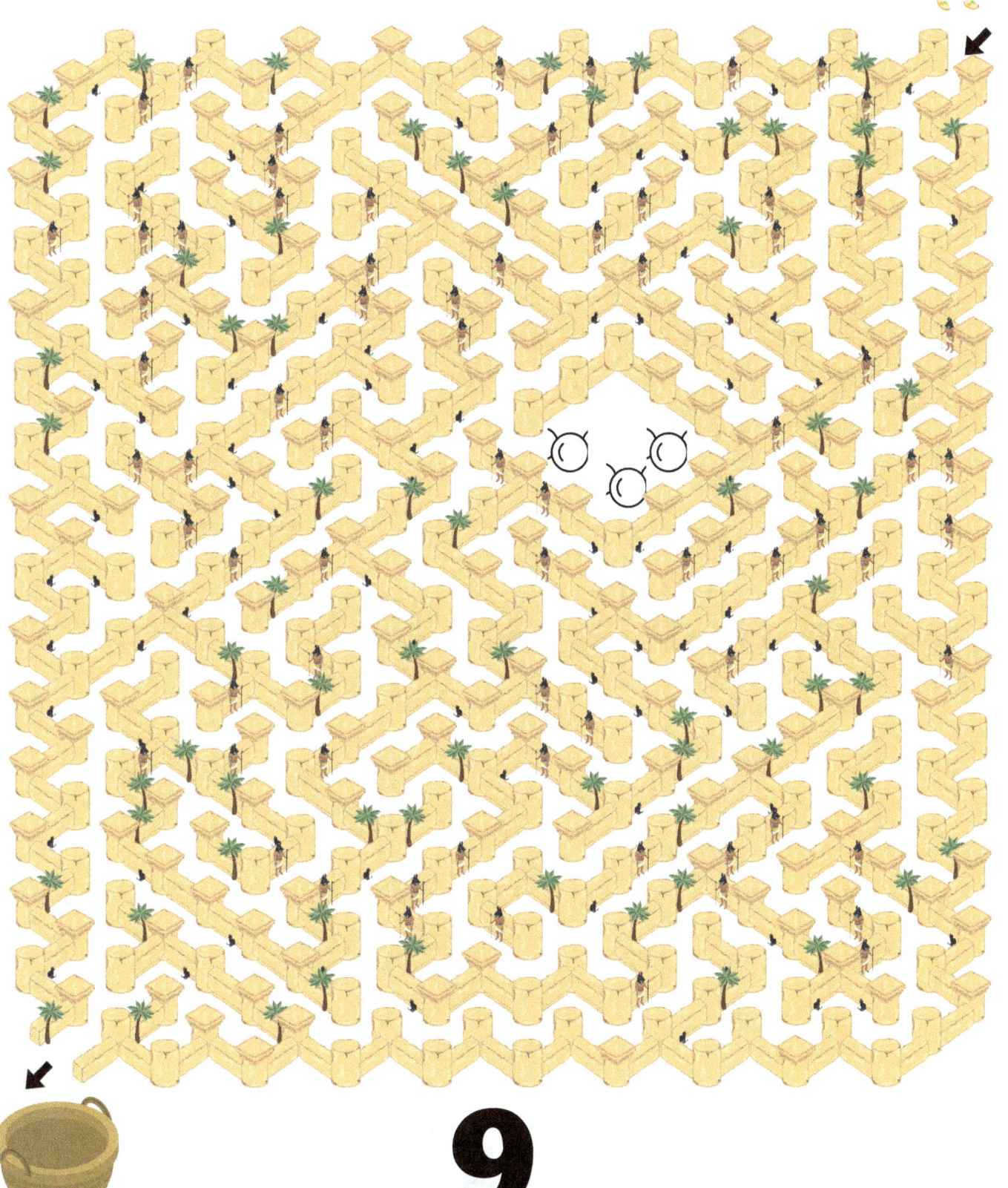

9

Return the pieces to Nala and head towards the Nile River where the real adventure begins!

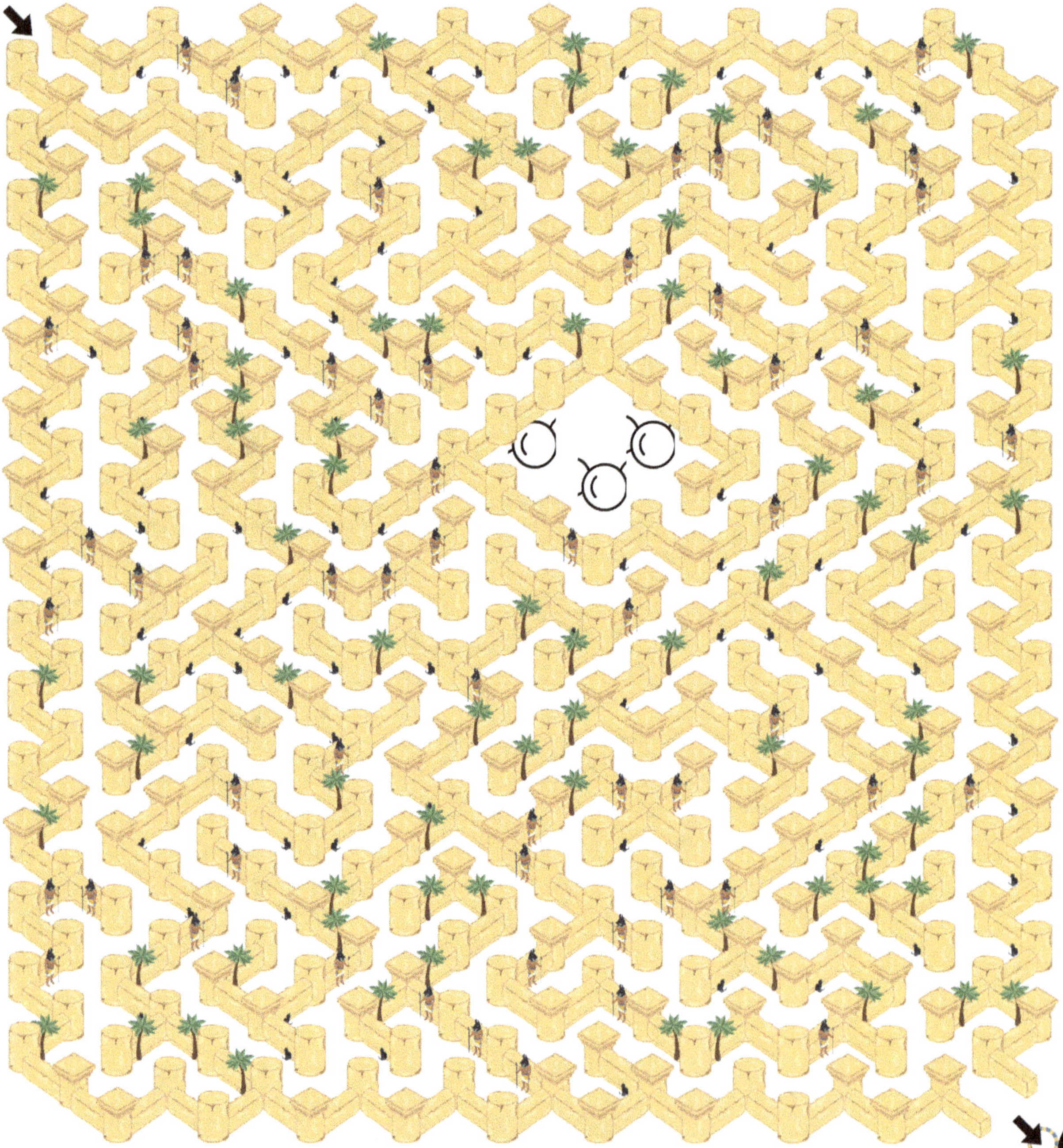

10

The only way across the Nile is by boat, so help Kavi and Henna find a friendly fisherman to get them across.

11

Faruu the Fisherman is here to save the day! The only problem is he has forgotten where he put his oar. Have a look in the crops and see if you can find it.

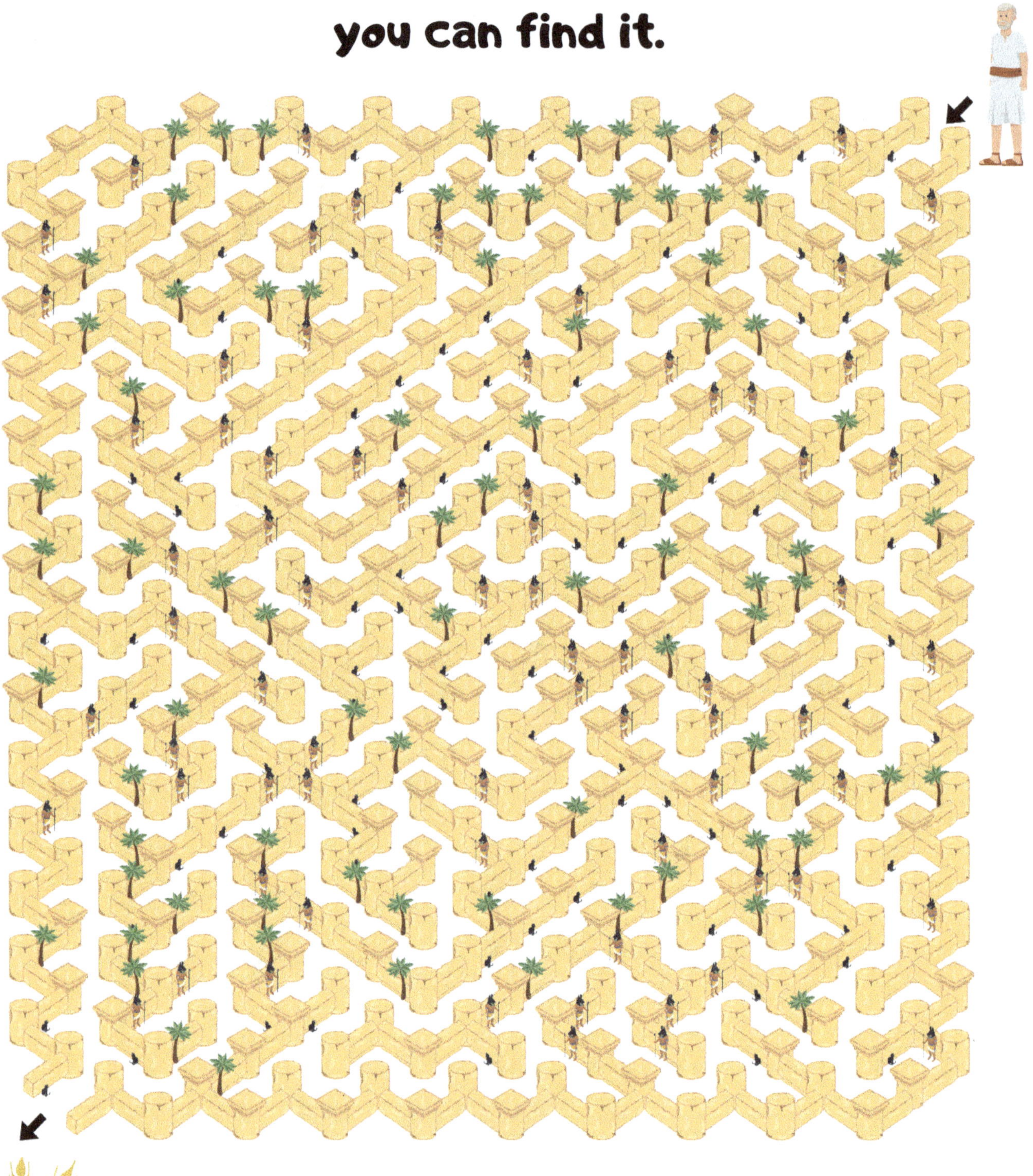

12

Faruu has found his oar floating in the river. Help him see if it's safe to grab...

13

Watch out! A crocodile! While Kavi and Henna distract it with some food from the markets, help Faruu go fetch the oar.

14

All aboard! The boat is now ready for travel. Help Faruu make his way across the Nile past all the other boats.

15

You've made it across! Now help Kavi and Henna get to Giza where their Dad, the Pharaoh, is building a giant pyramid. The trail of bricks will help guide you.

16

Ouch! A sandstorm has suddenly hit and it's hard to see! Watch out for the pile of bricks as you find somewhere to take cover. Quick! In that tunnel!

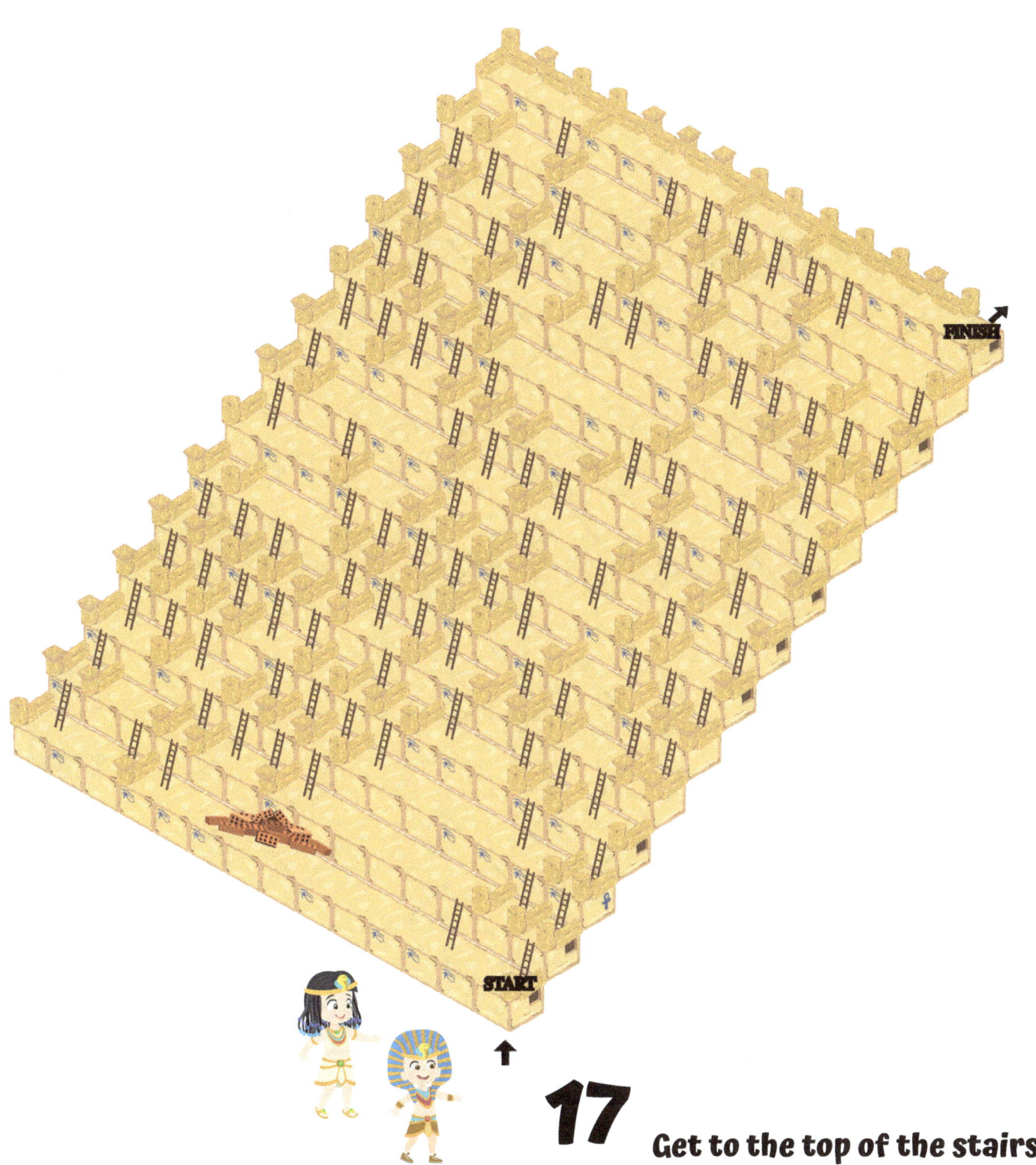

17

Get to the top of the stairs

Kavi and Henna find themselves in a secret tunnel. Help them make their way through so they can investigate some more.

18

At the end of the tunnel they find an empty tomb that has just been raided by thieves. They must let their Dad know! Collect any leftover statues or jewellery on the way out.

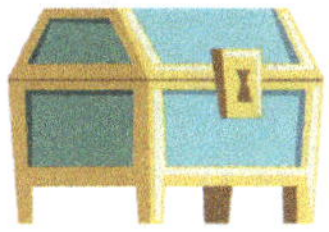

19

Oh no! A snake is blocking the way out! Use your flute to put it to sleep and get out of there!

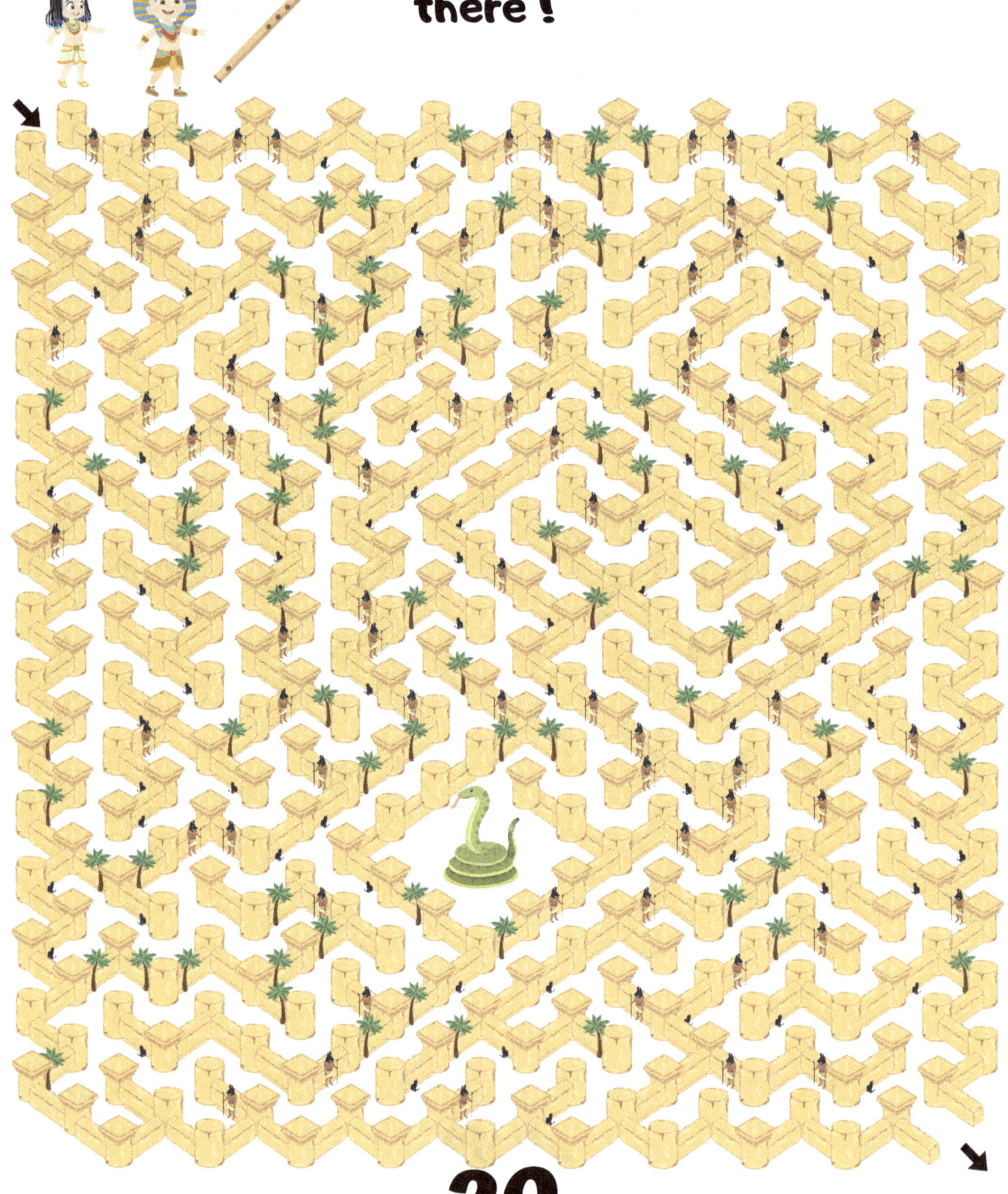

20

Now that the sandstorm has stopped, help Kavi and Henna follow the bricks all the way to the Great Pyramid of Kufu.

21

Weaving through the builders, go to Kufu so they can tell him about the tomb robbers.

22

As you make your way back to the tunnel, the Pharoah receives important news. Get everyone back to the royal palace ASAP!

23

The enemy's army is much closer than they thought! Have Kufu round up all the soldiers and their horses.

24

To give good luck to the Pharaoh and his soldiers, help Kavi and Henna collect 3 lucky charms to give to them: an ankh (symbol for good luck), a scarab beetle (a symbol of power), and the Eye of Horus (a symbol of protection).

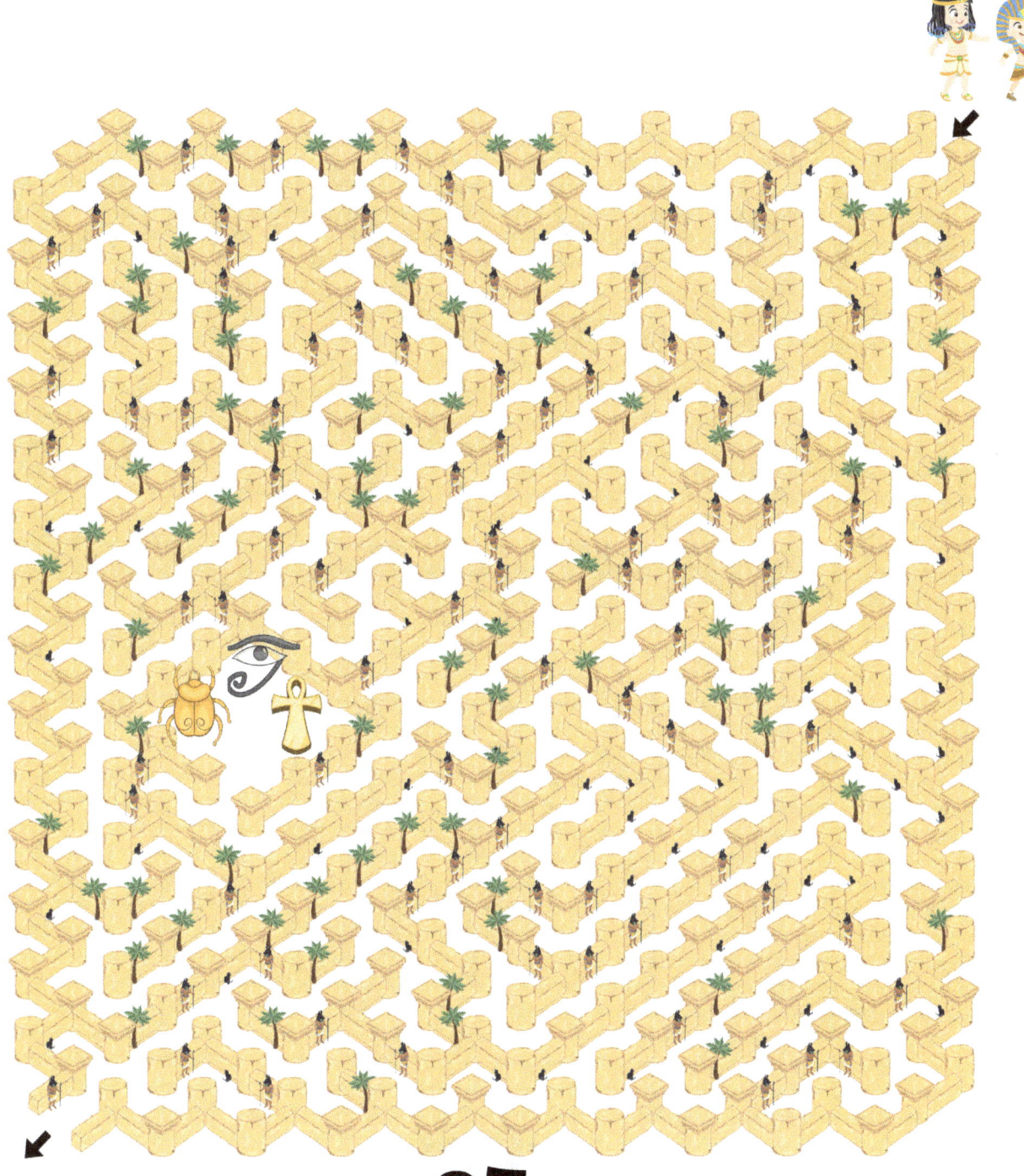

Now Queen Henu, wife of Pharaoh Kufu, needs to collect some of Egypt's finest food, drink and clothing to offer to the Falcon God of War, Montu. Help her gather them.

The battle has started! Grab a bow and arrow and help guide Pharaoh Kufu's chariot towards enemy soldiers. Don't get hit!

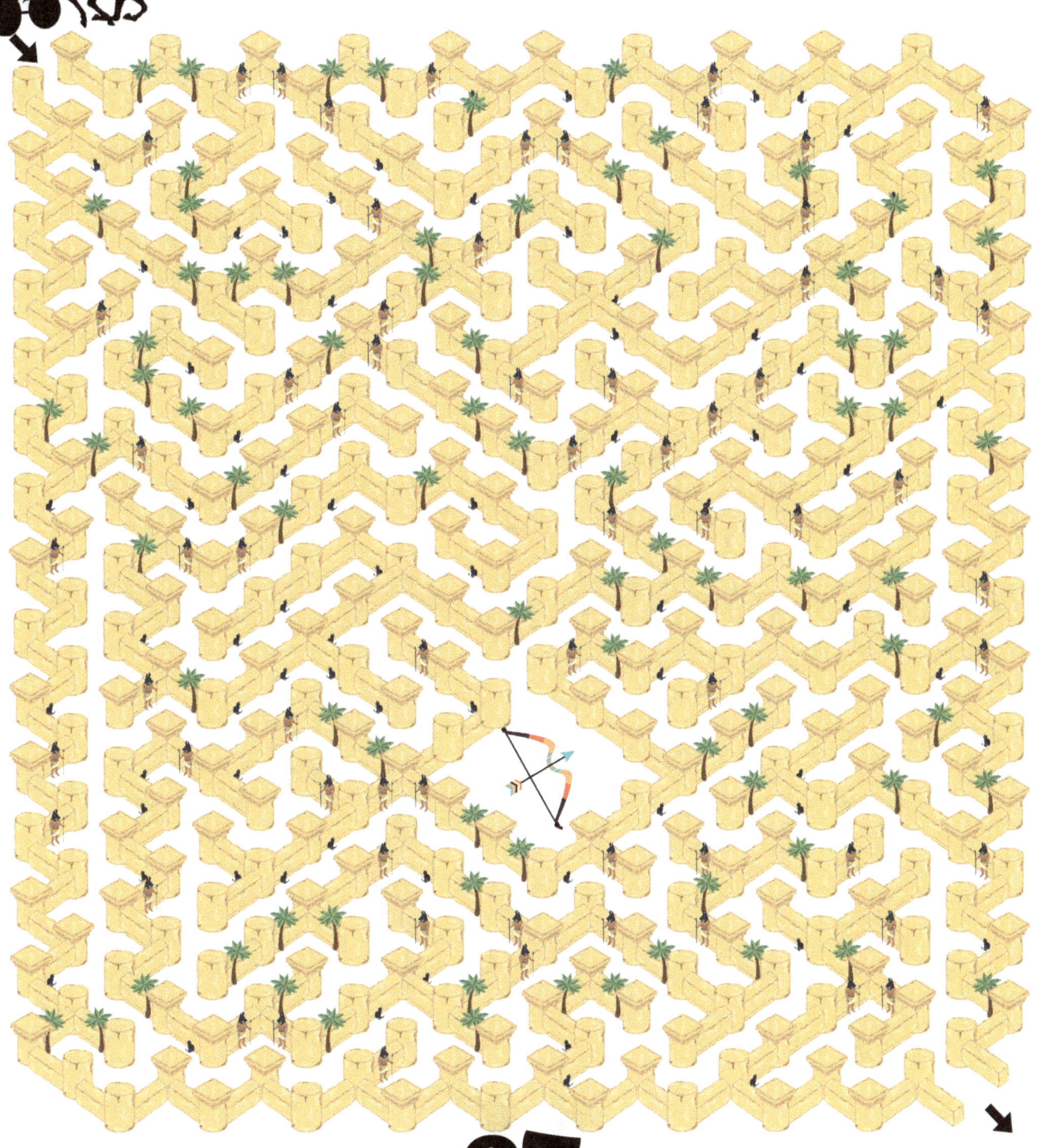

27

After a long battle, Egypt takes the victory! Help Kufu collect all the swords and shields from the ground, and then head back to town.

28

Everyone has heard of the victory and is out celebrating in the street! Help Kufu make his way through the crowds to find his family.

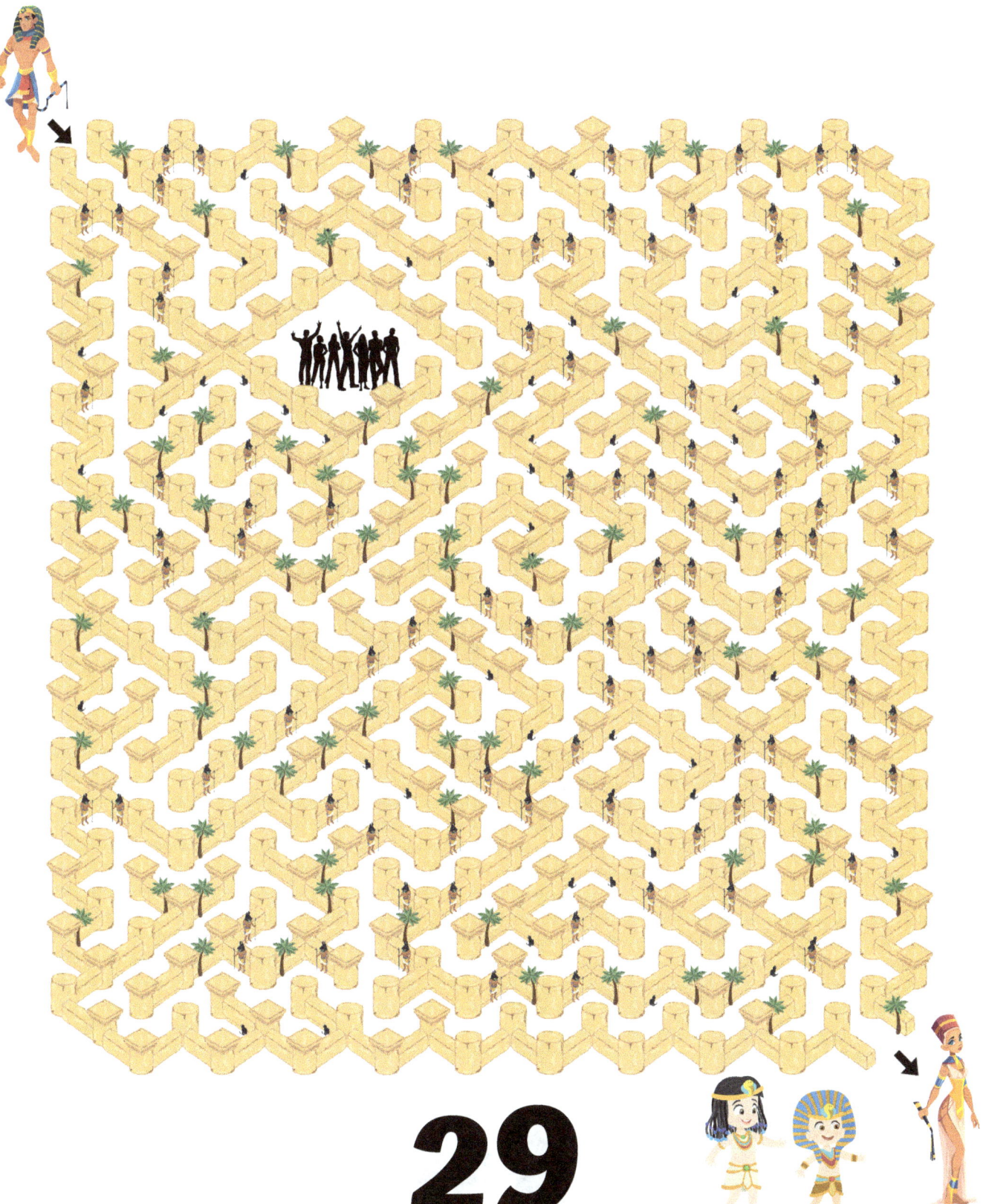

29

Now that they are reunited, and the day is done, it's time for a feast! Help Kavi and Henna collect the ingredients.

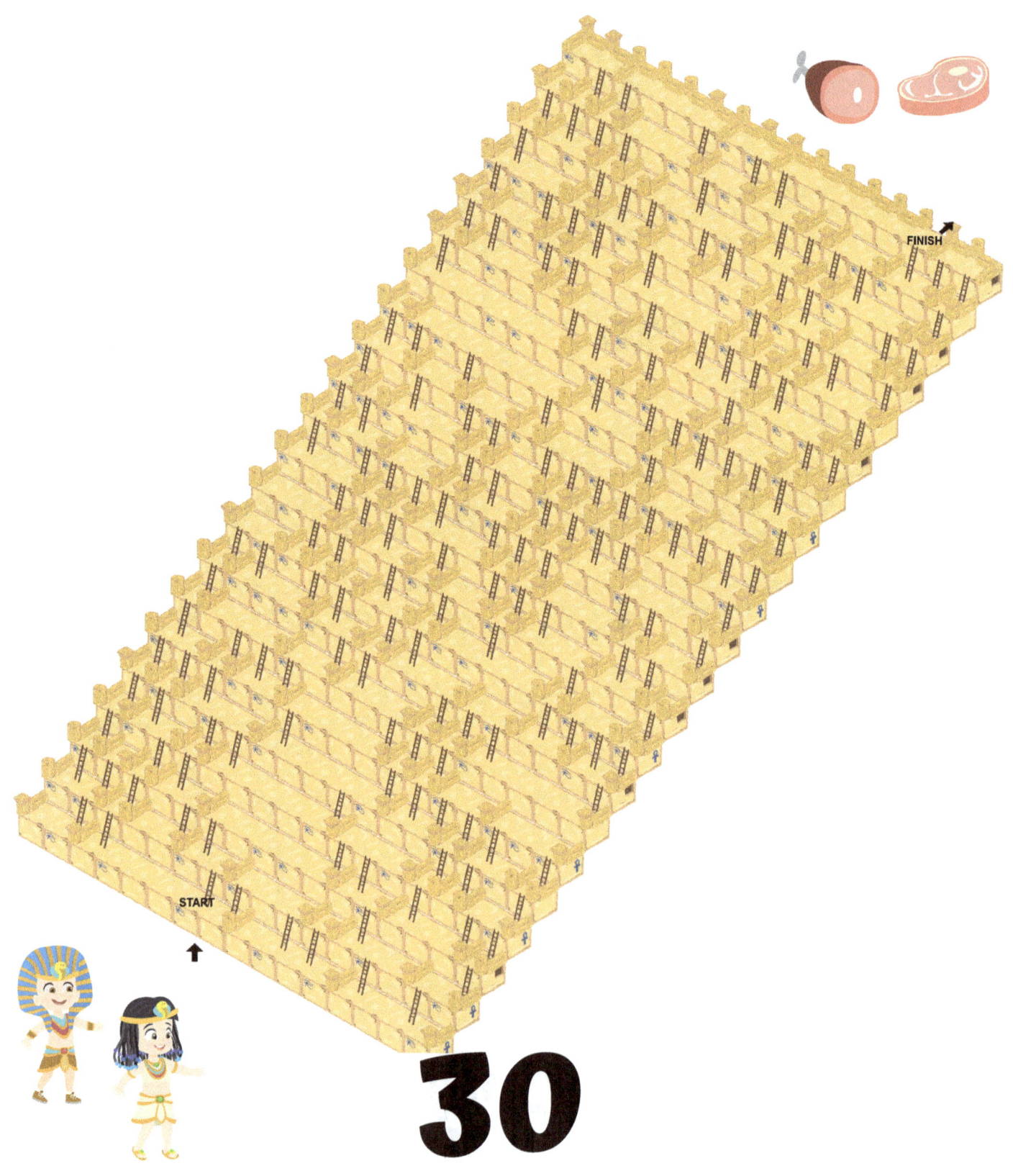

30

Guide everyone back home where they can share stories of their crazy adventures from that day.

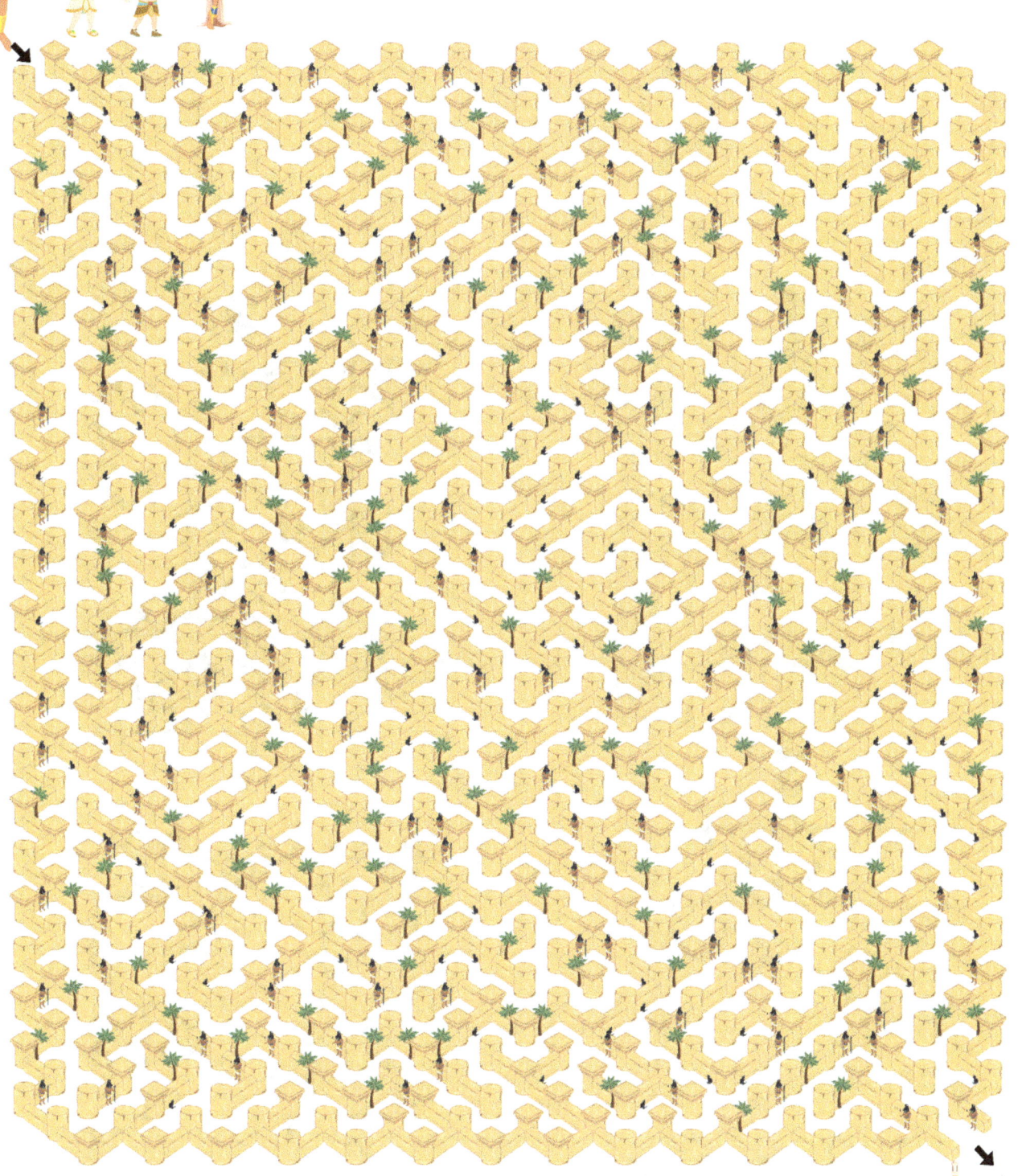

Solutions

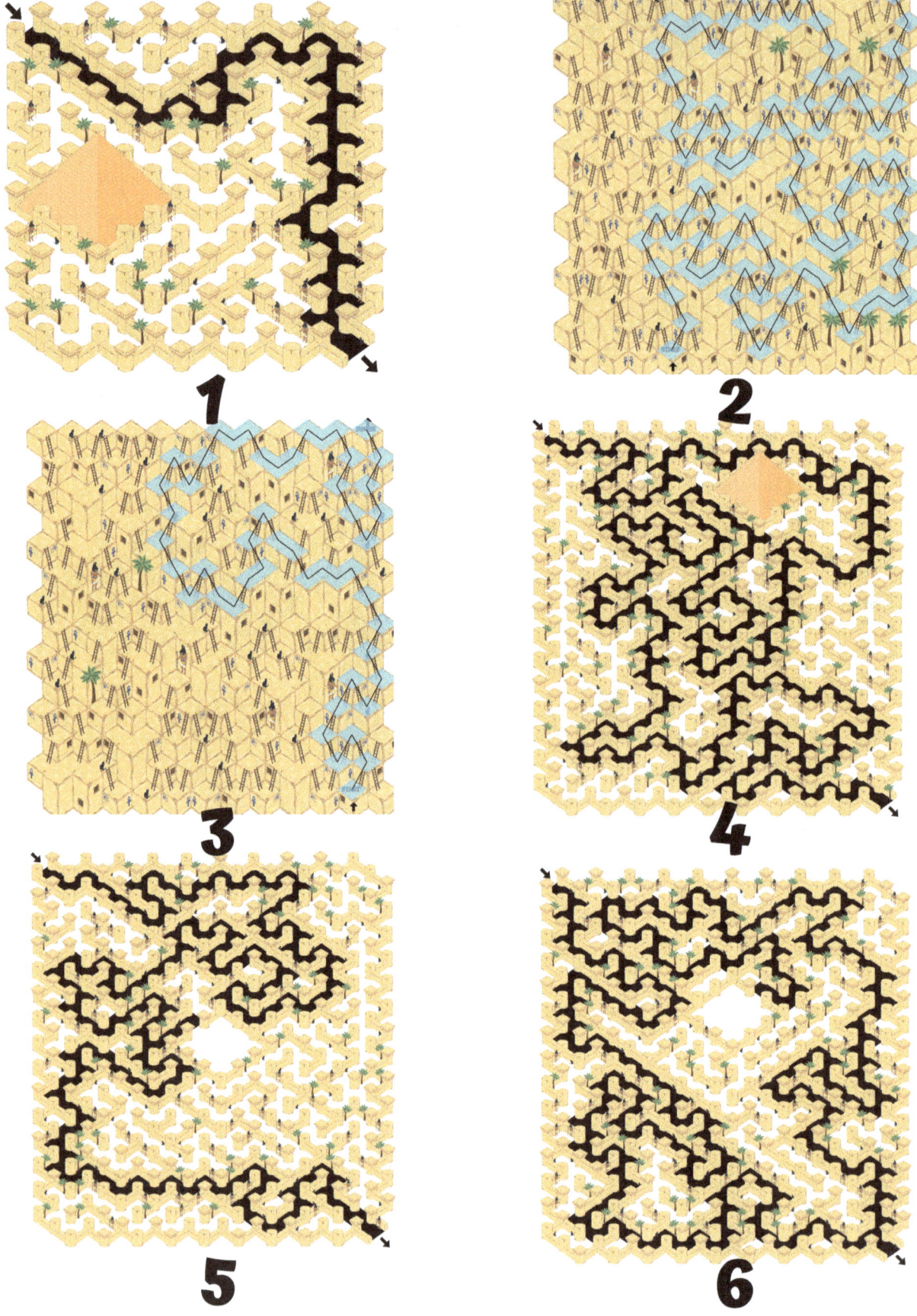

Solutions

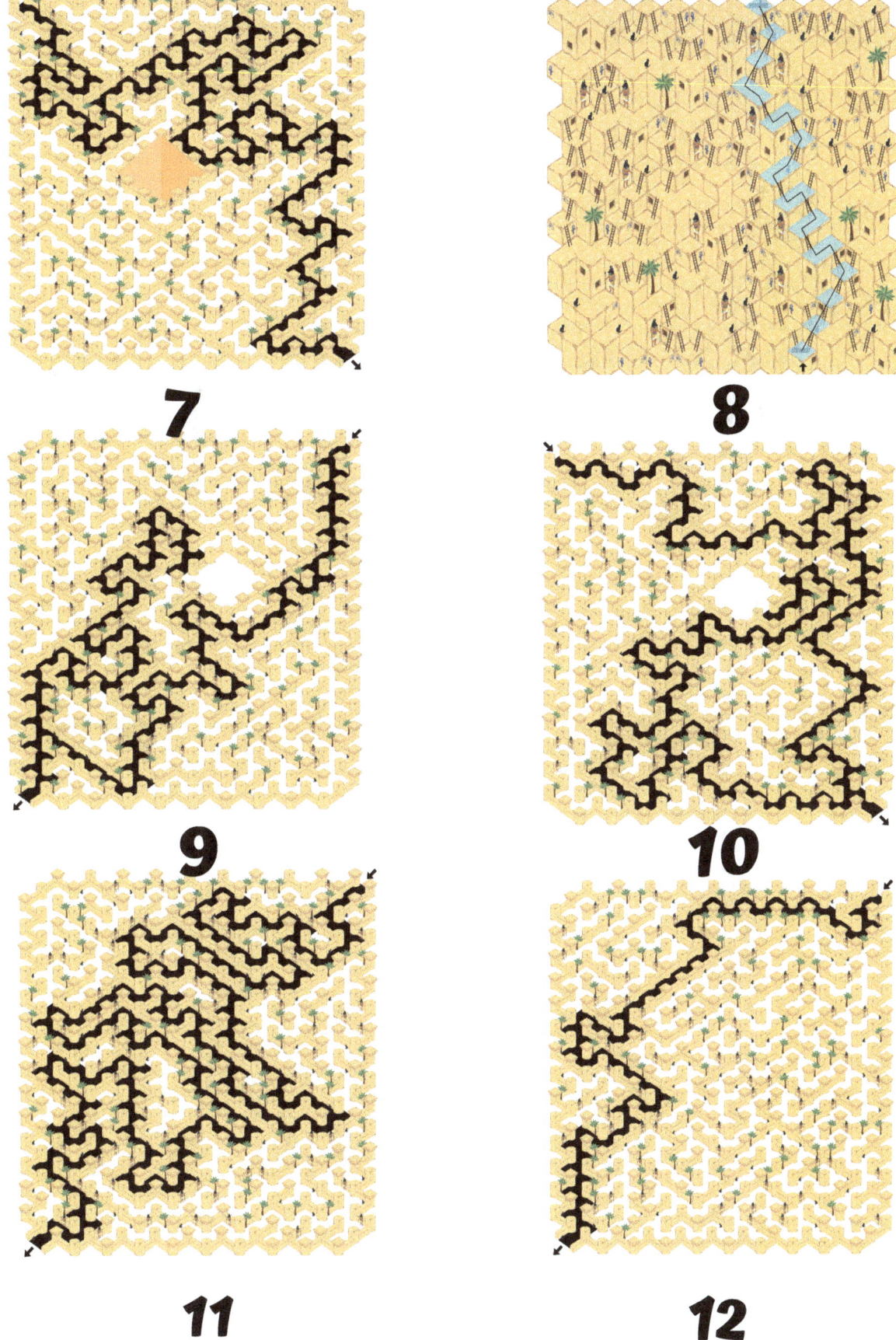

7

8

9

10

11

12

Solutions

Solutions

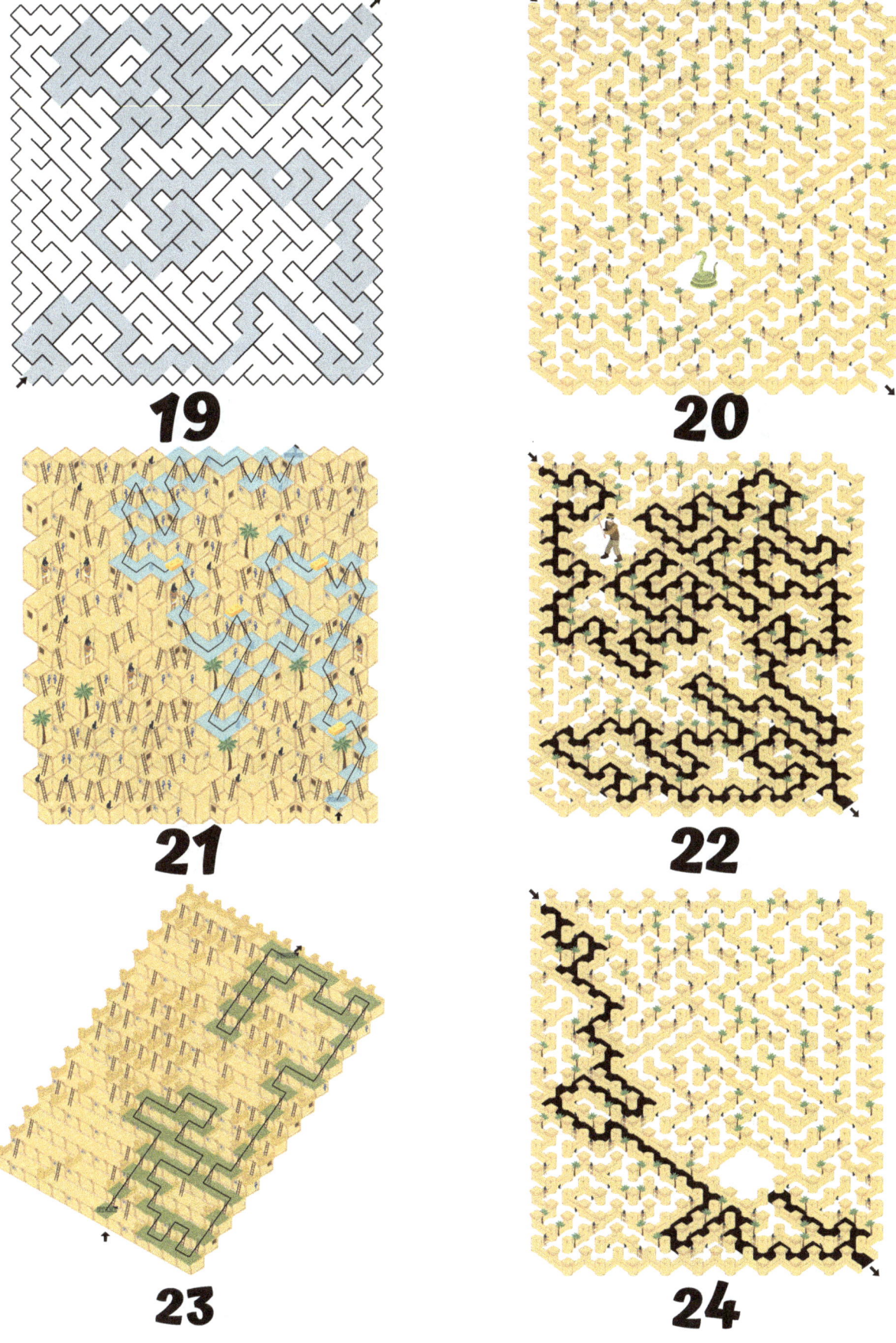

Solutions

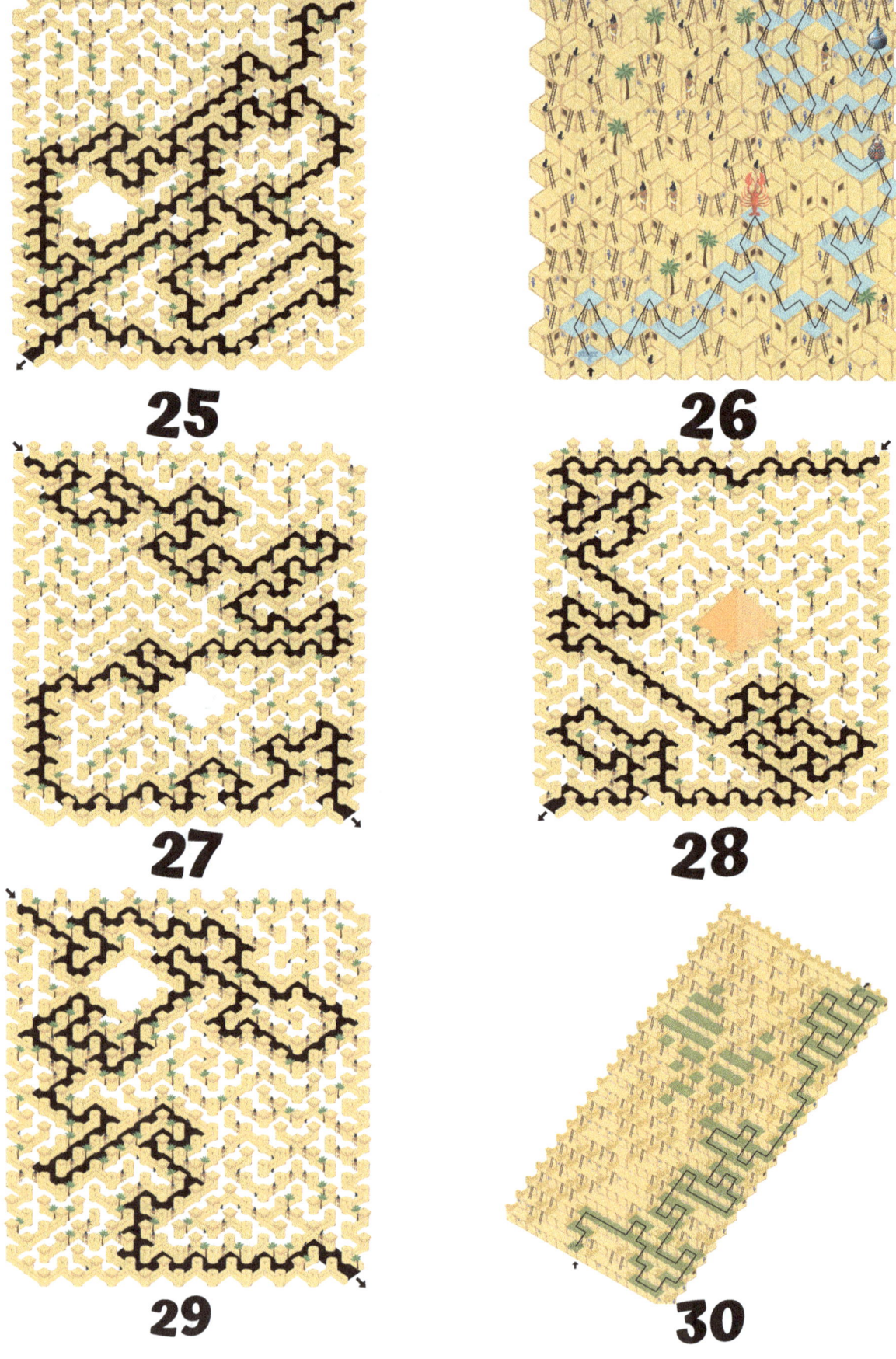

25

26

27

28

29

30

Solutions

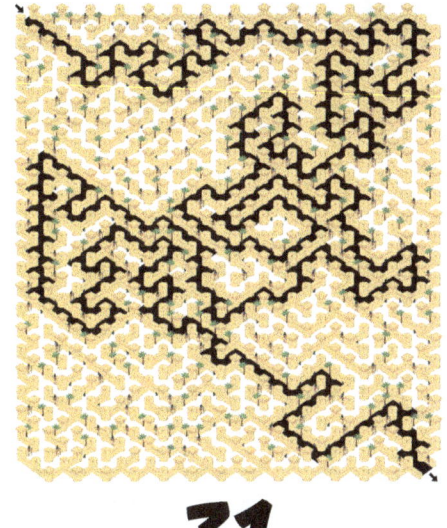
31

We hope you loved the mazes. If you did, would you consider posting an online review?

⭐⭐⭐⭐⭐

This helps us to continue providing great products, and helps potential buyers to make confident decisions.

For more mazes, find our similar titles

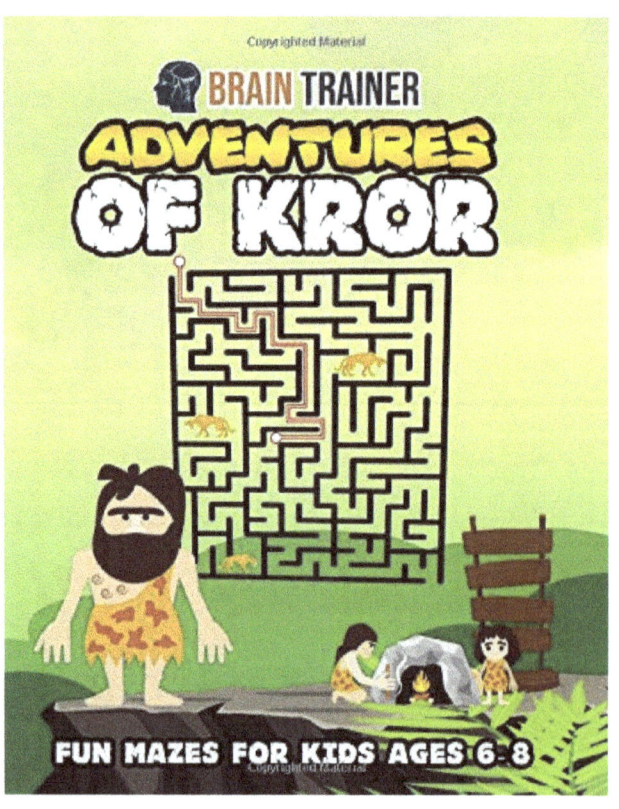

www.ingramcontent.com/pod-product-compliance
Lightning Source LLC
Chambersburg PA
CBHW081340080526
44588CB00017B/2692